American Robins: Spring Is Here

Photos and Poems
by
Dwayne Cole

American Robins: Spring Is Here
ISBN: Softcover 979-8-89532-005-1
Copyright © 2024 by Dwayne Cole

All rights reserved. No part of this book may be reproduced or transmitted in any form or by any means, electronic or mechanical, including photocopying, recording, or by any information storage and retrieval system, without permission in writing from the publisher.

Parson's Porch Books is an imprint of Parson's Porch & Company (PP&C) in Cleveland, Tennessee. PP&C is a self-funded charity which earns money by publishing books of noted authors, representing all genres. Its face and voice is **David Russell Tullock** (dtullock@parsonsporch.com).

Parson's Porch & Company *turns books into bread & milk* by sharing its profits with the poor.

www.parsonsporch.com

American Robins: Spring Is Here

Preface

> Beloved of children, bards and Spring,
> O birds, your perfect virtues bring.
> Your song, your forms, your rhythmic flight,
> Your manners for the heart's delight. . ..
> —Ralph Waldo Emerson

This is a book about the most beloved bird of North America. Its central purpose is to become one with the beauty and wonder of nature. In the beauty and wonder of robins, I am no longer rooted in earth. I have gained wings to soar in blue skies, one with all things.

While it is a book for all ages, it is primarily designed to be used with children through adolescent age to give them roots and wings. Many of the poems were first used with our children and grandchildren to help them grow in beauty and wonder, and to help them see that all of life is precious.

Introduction

    Let yourself be drawn
    By the stronger pull of that
    Which you truly love. —Rumi

All through the long Alaska winter, with 11 feet of snow, I held on to this truth—Nature's great gift is that spring always comes, bringing new visions of hope. Spring robins come with good news.

    Of all the spring birds
   Robins are best messengers
    Yard fills with magic

The arrival of two robins often signifies the beginning of the courting and mating season. They do not mate for life, however, they often return to the same place and mate for another season.

> I must confess
> Our hearts are captivated
> Beauty of robins

Robin Limerick

Once two robins came to our yard to play.

They announced, "Spring is on the way."

Grandchildren danced with joy.

They were like a windup toy.

Oh what a happy delightful day!

(A limerick is a five-line poem that consists of a single stanza. The first, second and fifth lines end in a rhyme. The third and fourth lines are shorter and end in a rhyme. The subject is a short tale or description. Many limericks are funny. See the Glossary at the end of this book on pages 76-77 for the definition of the different kinds of poems used in this book).

Bird baths help attract robins to our yard.
Robins like to bathe often,
more than other songbirds.

Sing Joyful Spring Sonnets

Winter's eleven feet of snow has melted.
Having robins in our yard this morning.
Spring jonquils are blooming in the garden.
What good news can I hope for now?

Flowers are kissing the pearl dew drops.
Robins have woven a nest from dry grass.
With a deep love that is faithful and true.
What good news can I hope for now?

To sit and dream new adventures.
Make our world well, as new as spring.
What good fortune can I hope for now?

The magic of Spring has come along.
Robins are hopping, raising their family.
All nature is singing a joyful song.

Spring Robin Sonnet

Spring jonquils and American robins,

add in the mix, a silver birch tree.

Grandchildren a Bob Bob Bobbing.

Summer vacation, and all are so free.

Robins and jonquils and our true love,

live on in our memory and never die.

Our love is sealed by angels from above.

Spring robins do not tell us a lie.

Nature's values are truth, beauty, and love.

Values of society since Plato in ancient Greece.

At Jesus' baptism, the Spirit came as a dove.

We feel love in Jesus' tender teachings,

in Spring jonquils and American robins—

In grandchildren a Bob Bob Bobbing.

Crabapple blossoms
And Spring Robins belong together—
Messengers of Hope.
Both One on the tree of life.
Cheer up, cheer, cheer, cheer up!

(The last line of this tanka is how some people hear the robin chirping song.)

A Short Robin Story

For the last 12 years, I have lived with a view of snow capped mountains and trees wearing bronze britches. I have walked in these nature settings an average of 5 miles a day. Wildflowers with a beauty too deep for tears have been abundant along my path.

I have locked eyes with bears, moose, and wolves. Little songbirds have added their praise, calming fears.

Each spring, on my walks in the foothills of the Chugach mountain range, I have encountered American robins. I have heard them chirping in the twilight and at dawn—Cheer up, cheer, cheer up.

I have watched them fly around my yard from silver birch trees to elderberry bushes, scouting out a territory for raising their young.

One afternoon when the last pile of snow had melted and the silver birch leaves had grown to the size of the little brown squirrel's ears, I saw a robin bringing straw to my deck. I looked up to the roof eave hanging over my deck, and saw straw hanging from a box-like light fixture.

For the next few days, I watched as a female robin wove a cup shaped nest. She started with long strands of coarse grass and then weaving smaller and smaller strands. Between the last few strands she placed mud gathered from the garden beds in our yard. Before the mud dried she shaped the inner part of the nest in the round shape of her body.

The nest is in the shape of a cup.
She lined the nest with moose hair and fuzz from the cottonwood trees.

The nest was ready for her to start laying her sky-blue eggs. I eagerly watch this miracle of nature with awe and wonder, dropping to my knees like Moses in front of the burning bush, drawn into the incredible magic of the tree of life—the dawning of the ages. Life was emerging as real as the growing buds on the crabapple trees.

Mother robin sitting on nest. Five eggs this morning. The eggs will be hatched in about 2 weeks, and the baby birds will grow feathers in next 2 weeks.

> Mother robin sitting on eggs
> Warmly incubating them
> Mothers are awesome

I'm an 84 year old lover of birds,
Who likes Summer solstice in Alaska.

Land of the midnight sun, all day sunlight.
American robins raising their young.

Red breast full of faithful and true love.
Heart's delight. Alleluia, alleluia!

A note on privacy: As a long-time bird watcher, I have learned the importance of privacy. I try not to invade the privacy of nesting birds. However, in this case, one might say the robins invaded my privacy by building their nest over the sliding glass door to my deck. My wife and I like to sit on our deck in our Cracker Barrel rocking chairs, especially after a long winter of heavy snow.

The robins must have observed us coming and going from our deck. Did they know we would not harm them? We still tried to grant them privacy as much as possible.

I even stopped putting out bird seeds and peanuts that might attract raptor birds like magpies and Steller's jays during the nesting period.

Some of the pictures could be taken from windows and doors with curtains slightly parted. I also used at times the Joby TelePod extension pole with the Bluetooth remote clicker to photograph nest when mother robin was out doing her personal business. We seemed to get along fine. The nesting time was successful.

A Most Famous Robin Poem

If I can stop one heart from breaking
I shall not live in vain
If I can ease one life the aching Or cool one Pain
Or help one fainting Robin Unto its nest again
I shall not live in Vain.
        —Emily Dickinson

A Most Famous Bird Quote

"A bird does not sing because it has an answer, it sings because it has a song."
   — Maya Angelou.

> I write poems,
> not to give answers—
> I have songs to sing.

Robin Visit Acrostic

R eturn of spring
O n wings of hope
B rings inspiration
I t's good to be alive
N ew adventures are on the way

Robin Tanka

Hear robins chirping
Happy as warm sunshine
Trees clap joyfully
My feet tap a little dance
Cheer up, cheer, cheer, cheer up

Keys to Identification of Robins

Size

American Robins are fairly large birds with a round body, long legs, and fairly long tail. Overall length is 9-11 inches. Wing span is 14-16 inches. Weight is 2-3 ounces.

Color

American Robins are gray-brown birds with warm orange breasts and dark heads. A white patch on the lower belly and under the tail can be seen, especially in flight.
Females have paler black heads than males.

Behavior

American Robins are fun to watch bounding across lawns in search of worms and insects. In fall and winter, they congregate in large flocks with as many as 100 to roost.

Bird baths are a draw for American Robins. Few birds bathe as often as they do. They also preen their feathers a lot. Sometimes they will clean almost every feather.

Songs

Robin songs are pleasant and often described as "Cheer up, cheer, cheer, cheer up." They add a note of joy to Spring.

Molting

Molting is the shedding of old feathers to grow new ones. The American robin has about 290 feathers, and they molt from July through September.

A Female robin normally lays 3-5 eggs in the nest, occasionally as many as 7. Sitting on the eggs, she incubates them for about 14 days. They may all hatch on same day. They grow feathers in the next 12-14 days.

During the first four days after hatching, the nestlings are fed by parents regurgitating food. Beginning on the fifth day they are fed small portions of earthworms. The next few days they are fed larger portions of worms and larger insects. After two weeks of care in the nest, they hop/fly from the nest. Robin parents feed them and teach them how to find their food, with fathers taking the primary role.

They eat more worms and insects in spring and summer; and berries and fruit in fall and winter. American robins can produce and raise up to three families of baby birds in a season.

American Robin
Collecting food for his mate
Heaven is here now

A Robin Haibun

I know spring is here when I see two robins hopping across my lawn. Pulling earthworms from the grass after a light rain. There could not be a more heart warming sight than the coming of bright orange breasted messengers of love.

I love these Robins,
who cheerfully sing to me—
Guardian angels!

        I hope you love birds too.

Shaped
Sky Blue Eggs
Poem

Robins
Woven nest
Five sky blue eggs
Mother incubating eggs
Father searches for worms
Spring is here indeed
Nature is magical
How I love
Robins

Robins
Red Breast
Filled with love
Faithful and true
From Heaven's realm
Loved ones appear
Guardian angels
Caring for us
Robins

The tv news channels
stream bad news

Tell that to the songbirds
wakened by the morning sun

Their music strikes joy
of being kissed by a parent

The sound is too sweet
to believe the bad news of despair

Rise and shine
Tell the good news

Faith, hope, and love
wins the day!

Guardian Angel Sonnet

Robins are a very special sight—
A visit from a loved one of your past.
Coming to tell you everything will be all right.
You can stop your worrying at last.

Your guardian angel is always near.
Watching over you with special care.
As faithful and true as your pet so dear.
Be adventurous and brave if you dare.

There could not be a more heart warming sight;
Mother robin incubating eggs day and night.
Father gathering food for mother and baby
birds.

The robin's red breast is full of love.
Your guardian angel is near as a dove.
Guardian angels come down from heaven.

Robin Stories From the Past

In this book of photos and poems about American Robins, I want to send a message of good luck to all children. The next time you see robins in your garden, be sure to spend some time with them. You never know what message they want to give you. These are some beliefs.

1. Robins are messengers from distant loved ones: When robins come to your yard, loved ones are near.
2. Robins bring good luck.
3. They are seen as symbols of new beginnings.
4. In some stories of myth, the robin is associated with the Norse god, Thor, the god of love and happiness.
5. Robins are our guardian angels.

There are variations of these myth stories in many cultures. Whatever beliefs people have, it is hard to deny the rich symbolism of the robin. From messengers of spring, good luck, happiness, and feats of bravery, this favorite bird continues to be highly loved. The next time you see a guardian angel robin in your garden, be sure to be still and listen. One never knows what good news a robin may have for you.

(This story used the word, myth; and the next sonnet begins with the word mythic. A myth is a story from the past. Some people think of myths as untrue, as lies even; but myths are more than true. Myths express true feelings that are hard to put in words.)

Nature Sonnet

Mythic bird poetry is an ancient art.
When the first humans were evolving,
birds were fully developed singing poets.
One with humans in seeing, hearing, feeling.

Smelling, touching, remembering ways.
These are poetic emotions of the soul.
All of nature has the desire to live.
Flowers lean toward the morning sun rays.

Birds and flowers remember in feeling.
Human poetry remembers in words.
All things in nature are kin, inter-related.

The world evolved one flower at a time.
Go into nature and rediscover your song.
Let poetry sing your feelings awake.

Bird photos and poems can lead us into a deeper awareness of oneness with the world of nature. In short, a poetic journey, or how to read bird stories.

       Poets laugh with the sun
       Illuminating mountains, clouds and trees.
       Love of nature illuminates me.

I grew up in nature with my fingers and toes in the soil of our farm in northwest Georgia, spending a lot of time exploring the woods and mill rock streams. Living and playing close to the land brings out a reverence for nature. My favorite movies were Tarzan of the jungles. I also grew up in a country church enamored by the tender teachings of Jesus filled with the birds of the air and flowers of the fields.

Retirement in Alaska is like going back home, back to nature. This second childhood with the wonder of grandchildren is filled with Harry Potter and Hogwarts. Tolkien's hobbits, elves, and Ents—Talking trees.

In Alaska, the last frontier, nature talked to me, saying, "Take my picture. Write a poem about me."

Many children have i-phones, and can take bird photos and write poems about them. Below are two types of poems that children can learn to write. See Glossary for definition of these and other types of poetry for children. I have also provided a few blank pages at the end of this book for you to write your poems (pages 76-79).

Haiku

I love these robins
Who cheerfully sing to me
Guardian angels

Sijo

A spring robin singing cheerfully.
Nest has been woven with loving care.

Five sky blue eggs have been laid.
Incubating with warmth fourteen days.

Both parents will bring daily food.
Form feathers in two weeks and fly from nest.

Beth, and I enjoy poetry and wanted to share verses with our grandchildren, as a way to nurture openness with the beauty and wonder of nature. The small haiku, has traditionally been seen as a good place to start teaching children a love of poetry. Haiku is a Japanese formatted short poem with three lines. The first and third lines have 5 syllables each, the second line has 7 syllables. The syllable count may vary slightly. The emphasis is on using as few words as possible.

Haiku uses inspiring nature scenes that enrich the lives of teacher and student. Our grandchildren's art work and poems helped us rediscover a child's wonder in our lives. Seeing the sparkle in their eyes helped us to see with the eyes of a child. The tears of joy washed away some of life's travel stains that cloud our vision. The wonder of a child blossomed anew in us, becoming fertile ground for tender teachings.

After haiku, sijo is a logical next step in teaching poetry. Sijo is a Korean style of lyrical poetry originally called "short song." Sijo resembles Japanese haiku in having a foundation in nature, but neither sijo nor haiku are limited to nature as subject. Sijo has three lines with 14-16 syllables in each line, for a total of 44-46 syllables. The count may vary slightly as in haiku. In sijo, there is a pause in the middle of each line, so in English they are sometimes printed in six lines instead of three.

(For more poems and information on haiku and sijo, see my books, Heart Haiku and Heart Sijo).

Haibun

Two robin eggs have hatched. Mother robin ate the shells while she was keeping the baby birds warm under her wings. After laying five eggs, the mother robin is depleted of calcium. She eats the shells to replenish those needed minerals.

Two baby robins
Hopefully, three more to hatch
Spring and Summer magic

(Haibun is a Japanese form of poetry that begins with a prose statement, followed by an haiku).

Three baby robins
Good things come in threes
Beauty, Wonder, Love

Baby robins growing
Feathers are coming on fast
What a miracle!

Robin Haiku

I must confess
My heart has been captivated
By beauty of robins

Robin Sijo

Robin nestling new-born chicks.
Safe as Noah's ark, wrapped in love.

After five days robins have eyes open.
Dazzling star light shining.

All of life is seen with new eyes.
Nature moves toward Beauty.

Male robin keeping watch
Some raptor birds raid nest
eating eggs and hatchlings

Some Raptors in Alaska

1. Sharp-shinned hawks
2. Red-tailed hawks
3. Rough-legged hawk
4. Northern Harrier
5. Northern Goshawk
6. Merlin
7. Owls
8. Eagles
9. Magpies
10. Steller's Jays

Humans and their use of pesticides are by far the greatest enemy of all birds, especially robins.

Mother's Visit

I woke this morning from a dream about robins. This was not unusual for me when I am working on a new poetry book. It happens often. When I was working on my book, The Bible: A Poetic Journey, I often woke with poetic dreams bouncing up and down the corridors of my soul.

Carl Jung says that dreams come from our inner psyche, our inner consciousness; and our personal consciousness is shaped by what we think about the most. I have spent the last few months totally consumed by spring-time robin visits. American robins are the best harbingers of spring.
One of the main myths about robins is that our loved ones come to visit us in the robin's activities.

This I know: My dear mother came to me in my dream. She said to me, "Dwayne, did you know that on the day you were born a robin came and sat on the window sill of my bedroom?" I, like all of my six sisters and six brothers, was born at home; delivered by our family doctor.

In my dream, I was overwhelmed by a deep feeling of love. Our mother never read the Confessions of Saint Augustine, but she knew one of Augustine's gifts: "God loves each one of us as if we were the only one to love." My siblings and I, all felt that love in our parents.

Each time I see the mother robin sitting on her nest incubating the five eggs, I will feel my mother's presence. Each time I see the male robin hopping in our yard gathering food for the young robins I will feel my father's tender care.

Oh seeker, these thoughts have such
a power over you. Make you happy. —Rumi

    Oh nature lover
    move from darkness to light
    Spring robins bring joy

    Mother seeking food
    Makes your heart very happy
    Such power of love

    Father Robin
    Finding food for young in nest
    Parents are awesome

COVID-19 Pandemic

From foreign lands it journeys
O'er land, sea, and air by plane
To wreak its deadly havoc
Followed by demons of fear

Death is its game
Daily outbreaks are counted
Deaths counted by cities and states
Political careers rise and fall

Blaming others is the game
Medical science pushed into back room
Obvious rules of washing hands
Wearing a mask still denied by many

The virus spreads each succeeding day
Mutating in many expected ways
How and when shall this scourge end
Keep your mask fresh and clean
Wash your hands often

Spring robins will come with news
We yearn for a new spring
Write poems of Hope
To heal our broken world

Of all the spring birds
Robins are best messengers
Yards fill with magic

(I could not write a poetry book for children without having a poem about the impact of Covid-19 on the lives of our children. All children have been drastically affected. I write the poem not to create fear, but to offer a message of how the robin brings hope of healing and new beginnings.)

Bird Evolution

Birds first evolved with wings of skin stretched between one elongated finger and their flanks. About 150 million years ago they began to turn into a much more aerodynamic feathered creature. The bird was born.

Human Evolution

Homo sapiens, the human species, is believed to have first evolved in Africa around 300,000 years ago. The human lineage began to evolve from chimpanzees around seven million years ago. We have fossils of Homo sapiens that date back to 300,000 years ago.

In the Bible, the Book of Genesis says that God created everything in 6 days. Birds were created on the 5th day, and humans were created on day 6. That was written about 3,000 years ago, prior to modern science. It is a beautiful story (myth) with the purpose of giving praise for the beauty and wonder of life.

"I tell you not to worry about your life. Don't worry about having something to eat, drink, or wear. Isn't life more than food or clothing? Look at the birds in the sky! They don't plant or harvest. They don't even store grain in barns. Yet your Father in heaven takes care of them."
—Matthew 6:25-26

Power of Bird Stories

Let yourself be drawn by the stronger pull of that
which you truly love. —Rumi

Bird poetry can inspire us to be more loving to others.

Some of the bird poems in this book have factual origins,

while others are fictional and somewhat humorous.

Bird stories can explain the world

and our experience in the world.

You can feel power in spring robin visits—

A feeling of discovery, making you want to take wings

and soar in blue skies.

Bird poems are songs of the universe,

singing us awake. When I watch spring robins,

I dance to the music of the spheres.

I wake to the music of angels singing—

God cares for the birds,

and God cares for you and me.

Praise be to God!

Value of Watching Birds in Nature

(For parents, grandparents, and all teachers of children.)

We spend time with birds in order to understand our lives in the natural world. We become a part of what we think about. We are actively becoming a part of nature. Participating not as object but as subject.
The overriding purpose is to become one with nature. In the eyes of the robins lighting in my yard for insects,
I see stars twinkling—I see a spinning universe. In this encounter I understand myself better. This interaction with nature is for awaking a new self
understanding. In this sense, the purpose of bird poetry is self understanding. In observing the song birds, they become kin, heart birds, giving us wings. We see new possibilities of flying with them in blue skies.

Robin Haiku and Tanka

In every robin visit
I hear loving parents say
We are with you always

In the robins
Hopping across our yard
We sing of family
A song of faithful love
We will not leave you alone

"Look at the birds in the sky! They don't plant or harvest. They don't even store grain in barns. Yet your Father in heaven takes care of them.... Look how the wild flowers grow. They don't work hard to make their clothes. But I tell you that Solomon with all his wealth wasn't as well clothed as one of them". God gives such beauty to every thing that grows in the fields."
　　　—See Matthew 6:25-30

In the tender teachings of Jesus, birds and spring flowers belong together as signs of new birth, new beginnings.

　　　　　Being one with nature
　　　Birds and flowers yield beauty
　　　　　Sun and moon shines

Poetry is Being in Harmony with Nature.

Spring jonquils blooming
Robin gathering food for young
Hope is a robin visit

I have poems not heard
Singing of new beginnings
Spring robins are here

From mystical lands
Under bird egg blue skies
Robins bring hope

A Robin visit—
A Guardian Angel!
God's care from above.

Little robins come
To let you know I'm always here
I will never leave you

At dawn of new day
Robins singing cheerfully
Spring is here today

Robin visit brings
Light out of darkness
Hope out of despair

I'm that little robin
Hopping among garden flowers
Sit still and listen
Hear songs of faithful love
I will not leave you alone

Ode to Robin

Happy little spring robins
and their tender days
Touch my heart with love
Tuning me to kinder ways

Beauty and Wonder
visit us daily
Perfect pictures of God
Tender and Caring

Happy little spring robins
and their tender way
Touch my heart with love
Tuning me to God each day

Tell me, if you can,
How many songs the mother Robin sings—
When her eggs hatch.

The robin is my tuning fork,
for composing a morning psalm.
Let's all sing along!

Searching for Answers

I spent over a dozen years in college and seminary discovering questions and searching for answers.

Questions grow for years,
and we should not expect quick easy answers.

Some questions have the ring of centuries in them. Pilate asked Jesus—"What is truth?" (John 18:38).

Since first encountering this question in seminary, I have been a question mark walking in shoes.

Or maybe fishing waders pulled up to my rib cage— A walking question. What is truth?

I have known some people who were answers walking in soft comfortable house slippers.

They lived with easy answers that gave comfort. I run from these easy answer persons!

Understanding the question—What is truth! I am always trying to find an answer.

What is truth? What shape? Where are the answers anyway?

I wake everyday thinking, Today, I will find truth!

I see a glorious sunrise, My soul trembles in awe!

Is this truth?

I touch a dimple on my grandchildren's sweet face,
Smiles as warm as the earth's sun rise.

Is this truth?

After driving the grandkids to school,
I take a long walk in the Chugach mountains.

Wild flowers and spring robins
brighten my way!

Is this truth?

I remember Jesus' words: God cares
for the birds of the air and the flowers of the fields.

God cares for you and me.
All day I walk at the edge of knowing truth.

Looking, longing, touching,
in beauty, goodness, and love.

Looking for truth!

Maybe I will never know for sure what truth is,
but this day feels like an answer!

Robin Sonnet

Return of spring robins is such fun.
Intent on building nest and raising young.
Feathers of hope, illumined by the sun.
Flowers are blooming, spring is here indeed.

Gather as much straw as you wish.
Devour worms to meet your needs.
High on list is filling your water dish
and the seed tray with sunflower heart seeds.

I'll never forget the wondrous feeling
the first time you built your nest under my eave.
For sure, you sent my heart reeling.

Tell me how many songs the mother Robin
sings. When her love nest is full of baby birds.
Robins are my tuning fork: Let's all sing along.

BEAUTY AND KINDNESS TRAINING EXERCISE

The central purpose of this book is about growing in beauty and kindness. Poetry of beauty and kindness is relational. Life is about relationships from birth till death. Relational beauty and kindness come naturally in family and community, and flows in personal ways. Emphasizing the relational aspects of beauty broadens the definition, moving toward kindness. Spring robins inspire beauty and kindness.

Mindfully setting aside times to meditate on how we can better show beauty and kindness to robins can help us become more sensitive and responsive to others within our everyday circles and move to include all persons.

Find a quiet time each day to contemplate on what you desire for your family and yourself:

* To be safe and secure
* To be happy and at peace
* To have good health
* To be free from fear
* To have fun times for all in family
* To see beauty in all people, animals, and all living things

(Practicing this exercise daily would change our world.)

> The little robin
> comes with joyful good news
> God will care for you

Spring Cheer Sonnet

Building a robin nest is a love dance,
an heroic adventure, a song fest.
Announcing to all this is our chance.
We will protect it as Guardian Angel guest.

Feed and care for each with deep love.
Tell faithful stories to our young chicks.
With God's daily care from above.
Of all song birds, robins are my picks.

Feathers of hope illumined by the sun.
Fill my heart with warm family feelings.
Sharing with your family songs is such fun.

I love my American robin family.
Bringing the good news that Spring is here.
Let's all sing, cheer up, cheer, cheer, cheer.

A Summary Vision of Beauty

My vision for all children is that they grow toward beauty.
Seeing beauty in spring robins is a step in that direction.

Beauty is the key for understanding
the loving and generous heart beat of nature.

The inner nourishing of a kind spirit in every person
is one of the most important needs in our world today.

Beauty in one's heart is felt by the universe.
Yet, I am painfully aware of the chasm between this vision

and its ultimate expression in our world that is so divided.
Visions may be expressed in gentle words,

but they are more powerful when expressed in tender
actions.

Centered in beauty and kindness,
we can transform our world.

I am so hungry
I could eat a whole worm
Yummy in tummy

Father Robin feeding
Seven day young nestlings
Happy Father's Day

Baby robins grow rapidly. These are about 10 days old. Could leave nest in a few days. They are feathered except for their stomach. They are looking like their parents. As soon as they leave the nest, the father robin takes full responsibility for feeding them and teaching them to find their own food. This allows the mother robin to repair the nest and begin laying eggs for another brood. The parents may raise as many as three broods a season.

Parents were feeding
hungry nestlings fast and furious.
Loud thunder rumbling.
Lower the windows to the nest.
Under mother's wings secure.

The pounding rain storm
quietened; and went to rest.
Leaving a rainbow
uniting heaven and earth.
Guardian Angels watching over nest.

The baby robins, thirteen days after hatching, have flown from the nest. Papa robin has now taken the major role in feeding them, and teaching them to find their own food.

Robin Sonnet

Poets of all ages have celebrated robins.
Especially children, bob, bob, bobbing.
American Robin: Spring is Here.
Cheer-up, cheer, cheer, cheer.

Three little robins hopping in the yard
One robin said, "Hope I can find a worm."
The second little robin said, "Chugalug.
I just want to find a fat little bug."

The third little Robin said with a shrug,
"I don't want to eat a worm or a bug.
I want a tender little salad leaf."

Sang the father robin, "Oh good grief.
To grow big and strong and free.
you must eat all three, like me."

Robin Sonnet

Let the Robin sing a cheerful song
Never do these gentle birds any wrong
Every spring they arrive on time
With good news for my rhyme

American Robins, fairy tale birds
From the land of fly away fables
Looking eagerly all around
Spied father pulling a worm from ground

To witness a baby robin being feed
by father with tender loving care
Is a joy forever we dearly need

You cheered me with song
Filled my heart with love all day long
Little robin fly away home

(Father watching over juvenile robins).

Nature's Miracle

God will command angels to protect you wherever you go. —Psalm 91:11

One reason for watching robin beauties is
so the joy we see in them will become our joy;
and their beauty will become our beauty.

The sense of being
one with spring robin beauties
is Mother Nature's precious gift.

Robin beauty is nature laughing with us,
while moving us toward love for all people.

In nature we are all interconnected as one. One family caring for each other.

Said the Robin
to the little forget-me-nots
Love never forgets

A father robin
Hopping among forget-me-nots
Happy as he could be

When robins appear
Loved ones have come to visit
Love never forgets

Robin Sonnet

Walk around the yard lined with tulips
glowing in warm life giving sun so bright.
Letting my soul become one with the light—
Nature's enlightening soul of wonder.

Suddenly I hear a robin chirping so free.
On a limb high in the silver birch tree.
Beauty offered itself to my imagination.
Finding myself in the family of life.

What's it like to be one with birds singing—
Hear the good news of church bells ringing?
One with robins nesting under roof eave.

Enjoying the wild natural things today.
Dew catching sun rays with its pearls.
What will I do when the robins fly away?

        American Robin—
        Fly, fly away with my heart.

D. Cole

There is a saying, "You can tell a lot about a person by the company they keep." Pine grosbeaks and redpolls get along fine with robins. These song birds visited my deck and yard while robins were nesting.

Black-capped chickadees and nuthatches are friendly little birds and eat heart seeds from my hand. They also get along with robins; and they can nest in trees in the same yard.

(Getting them to eat seeds from your hand requires patience. Also, if you try this trick, be sure to wash your hands before and after feeding. Wash feeding trays often as well to keep down diseases.)

Because I cannot board
a flying saucer cloud
and fly to you.
You kindly fly to me.
My deck holds but just friends—
And visions of Eternity!

While some precocious older children will understand this
next poem, it is primarily written as a poem for parents,
grandparents, teachers, and all caregivers of children—

Contemplation of the intricacies of nature
and putting those wonder-filled subtleties
in poetry is indistinguishable from magic.
Combining science and the humanities
grounds that mystery in observable reality.

Expressing the supreme beauty
and truthfulness of nature lies beyond
the everyday meaning of words one finds in a dictionary.
Contemplating the little things in nature
gives new eyes and new ways of seeing the big picture.

In this sense, poetry is the expression
of the unseen message in the seen observable reality.
The birds are the poems,
and the poems are messages from unknown realms.

For the last decade, I have closely observed birds
coming from all parts of the world and landing on my
deck, some even eating sunflower heart seeds
from my hand.

Because I can not fly to you
You kindly fly to me.
My deck holds but just friends—
And visions of Eternity!

There is in visible bird wings
an invisible mysterious wisdom.
A fountain of joy and purity.
A tenderness that flows to me.

In this relational oneness,
I experience a hidden wholeness—
A union with all birds and all things.

The Poet of the world speaks
One in many,
many in One.

In the eyes of the little birds,
I see the spinning universe
revealing secrets about secrets.

Moving toward adventurous truth, beauty,
goodness, love, kindness,
and a peace that passes all understanding—
A union of all things as one.
One in many, and many in One.

Embracing and preserving this poetic beauty
can save our lives and save our deeply divided
world from destruction.

In summary, one of the greatest needs in our
modern world is to cultivate a reverence for all of
nature, all of life.

From a faith perspective,
God values all life and feels within God's own being
all lives. If God values even the worst within us,
we can also value all others.

The leaves are colorful now
The grass is turning brown.
The robins are out of town

Poets of all ages have celebrated birds
more than any other beauties of nature.
Both poets and birds sing songs.
Humans in all cultures dream of taking wings
and soaring in blue skies. The American Robin
is a symbol of this freedom and hope.

Conclusion

This book on American robins has been a poetic journey with our children and grandchildren to reveal nature's beauty and wonder. My nature poetry is a call for an adventure that embraces change and growth; and sees kindness as a force in the universe. To say that I daily help children grow more kind is to say that kindness is the reason for my existence.

Robins are known for building their nest in the shape of a cup.

Did I mention just
how much I love spring robins?
Cup filled with love!
Fill my cup to overflowing.
Fill my life with songs of praise.

Without doubt, the American Robin is one of North America's favorite birds. It can be seen in most of the United States at some time during a calendar year.
It is used on the two dollar bill of Canada, and is the state bird of Connecticut, Michigan, and Wisconsin.

Marvelous Mystery

The Robin is filled with mysteries so marvelous.
How they mate, build a nest, lay eggs, sit on the eggs for two weeks—Then the eggs become little robins!
Mother robin keeps them warm and feeds them, with father's help, for another two weeks, while they are growing feathers. The young robins defy gravity,
and hop/fly from the nest in search for food. Watching them, we laugh and dream of flying. Bowing our heads in awe often and singing praise.

>In May and June,
>the world around the robins explodes.
>Nature is marvelous

>Green grass, insects, and worms,
>jonquils, and tulip blossoms.
>Alpenglow sunrises and sunsets—
>Nature is marvelous,

(Juvenile robin sitting on fence rail)

In writing this book, I found my story to be filled with kindness. Can anything be more kind than robins caring for their young?

In Alaska, I live a meditative contemplative life, filled with nature's beauty and wonder. Watching the little robins being feed by their parents, I realize how marvelous life is!

Do you know how big kindness is?
Kindness can transform hatred into love,
wars into peace.

American robin poetry leaves a divine heart print
stamped on your words and actions.
Poetry is the life blood of change.

Nature Sings Sonnets

Snow capped mountains with green spruce trees.
Artist painting the sky. Robins are trilling.
We lie on the summer green grass while grilling.
Hearing soft music of honey-laden bees.

Nature's smell is as sweet as flowers.
I dipped my toes in the glacial stream.
Soul refreshed by draping bowers.
And time stood still as in a dream,

My love lies beside me. Arms around my neck.
The sun slips behind the golden trees,
and the silver moon came up silently.

Oh the wonder that comes in feeling
two earth bound bodies becoming one.
With nature singing the song of our being.

Robin Sonnet

Yard is full of robin life so free.
Just one month after five eggs are laid,
young robins are hopping in the tree.
Learning how to find food with aid.

After parents help each magical day,
defying gravity they will fly away.
After one or two years, the young will date.
Start their own family in tree by the lake.

Nature thrives on the desire to live.
Blessed by the sun, stars, and silver moon.
Having many wondrous gifts to give.

Photos and poems capture this wonder.
For children and bards not yet born
All will be Eternity one glad morn.

Glossary of Types of Poems in this Book

Acrostic: a poem in which the first letter in each line forms a word or words.

Free style poetry—Poetry that is an open form of poetry. It does not use consistent meter patterns, rhymes, or any musical pattern.

Haiku: A Japanese formatted poem that has three lines. The first and third lines have 5 syllables, and the second line has seven syllables. The emphasis is on brevity, and the syllable count may vary slightly. Nature is usually the subject. However, the subject is not limited to nature.
The third line is usually a surprise or ah ha
moment. Haiku is one of my favorite types of poetry. Haike is considered a good place to start teaching poetry to children.

Haibun: A poem that starts with prose and ends with a haiku. The prose is often autobiographical.

Limerick: A limerick is a five-line poem that consists
of a single stanza. The first, second and fifth lines end in a rhyme. The third and fourth lines are shorter and end in a rhyme. The subject is a short tale or description. Most limericks are funny.

Odes: An ode is a type of lyric poetry that originated in Ancient Greece. Odes are poems praising an event or individual, describing nature emotionally.

Photo poems: A photo that speaks without written words.

San dab: A sand dab is a short poem by Mary Oliver, named after the san dab fish. It is often just one line: Mother robins are awesome.

Shaped Poem: See egg shaped poem on page 19.

Sijo: A Korean style of lyrical poetry originally called "short song." Sijo resembles Japanese haiku in having a foundation in nature, but neither sijo nor haiku are limited to nature as subject. Like haiku, Sijo has three lines, with 14-16 syllables in each line, for a total of 44-46 syllables. The count may vary slightly as in haiku. In sijo, there is a pause in the middle of each line, so in English they are sometimes printed in six lines instead of three. If Haiku is a good place to start teaching poetry, sijo is the next logical step.

Sonnet: A Sonnet is a poem with fourteen lines that uses any of a number of formal rhyme schemes. In English a sonnet typically has ten syllables per line. However all definitions of poetry must be taken with a grain of salt. Historically, the poet has been granted freedom to alter syllable count, rhyme, and rhythm without reason. Free style poetry is popular today.

Tanka: A haiku with two additional lines of seven syllables each. Syllable count may vary slightly.

Lessons Learned from Caring for Birds

1. Seeing our oneness with the universe. We are all kin, related as one.

2. Kindness is reciprocal healing.

3. Being kind to birds is as important to children as it is to birds.

4. Caring for birds brings joy to all.

5. Bird watching inspires hope.

6. Gives birth to creativity.

7. Teaches poetry. Photos are poems. Poems are photos.

8. Learn the importance of thanksgiving.

9. Become more grateful.

10. Bird watching instills beauty, wonder, goodness, art, novelty, and adventure.

11. Seeing value in nature leads to seeing value in our lives and value in all people.

12. Learning that life is precious. This lesson alone would change our world for the good.

13. Instills ecological concerns, saving our world for future generations.

14. Caring for birds nurtures the soul, leading to an inclusive love of all humankind. Learning this lesson reduces violence in our world.

15. Contemplating in nature is not evading the contemporary problems of life. It is preparing our soul to go into the world to create positive change.

16. Caring for birds nurtures the experience of being alive—The song of the universe.

Your Response is Important

The following blank pages are intended for you to write your response to this book. You might want to express your thoughts in poetry.

I learned more from children and students than they learned from me. So, I would appreciate it if you would send me your response to this book.
Send to tadpolejr@aol.com

The list of my books on next pages were all born from my masters thesis:

HERMENEUTICAL THEORY IN TRANSITION AS REFLECTED IN INTERPRETATION: A JOURNAL OF BIBLE AND THEOLOGY (1947-1966);

and my doctoral dissertation:

BAPTISM AND THE LORD'S SUPPER IN THE GOSPEL OF JOHN: A HERMENEUTICAL INQUIRY.

This parentage is especially true of my book:

A Relational Hermeneutic of Kindness.

On the deepest level, all of my 50 year preaching ministry, published articles, Sunday School lessons, devotions, and poetry books were born from this parentage.

BOOKS BY DWAYNE COLE

(My wife, Beth, is a professional editor, and made major contributions to the 35 books I have published. I list mainly my poetry books here as aids in teaching nature poetry. Many of the poems in these books were first used with our children and grandchildren to help them grow along with the beauty and wonder of nature. For my other books see Parsons Porch Books, Barnes & Nobles, and Amazon).

American Robins: Spring Is Here

A Center that Holds: Adventures in Kindness

Alpenglow Miracles: Fire Dance of Wonder

A Prayer of Blessing: As You Go Remember This

A Relational Hermeneutic of Kindness

A Relational Trinity of Kindness

BEARS AND MOOSE OF ALASKA: Nature Poetry
Black-Capped Chickadees: Messengers of Good News
Clouds of Inspiration
Down on the Farm in Georgia: A Poetic Memoir
Dragonfly Magic
Gentle Galilean Glories: The Tender Teachings of Jesus
Heart Haiku: Alaska Inspired Photos and Poems
Heart Sijo: Alaska Inspired Photos and Poems
Kindness Is Every Step
Lone Leaf Dancing
Rainbows of Hope
Snowshoe Hare Beauty
Steller's Jay Blue Sway
TREES AND DRIFTWOOD: Poetic Ecology
When Flowers Speak, Listen
When Stones Speak
WINGS OF INSPIRATION